family favourite
vegetables

Bath • New York • Singapore • Hong Kong • Cologne • Delhi • Melbourne

D1633671

aubergine dip

ingredients

SERVES 6–8

olive oil

1 large aubergine,
    about 400 g/14 oz

2 spring onions, chopped
    finely

1 large garlic clove, crushed

2 tbsp finely chopped fresh
    parsley

salt and pepper

smoked sweet Spanish paprika,
    to garnish

French bread, to serve

method

1 Heat 4 tablespoons of oil in a large frying pan over medium–high heat. Add the aubergine slices and cook on both sides until soft and starting to brown. Remove from the pan and set aside to cool. The slices will release the oil again as they cool.

2 Heat another tablespoon of oil in the frying pan. Add the spring onions and garlic and cook for 3 minutes, or until the spring onions become soft. Remove from the heat and set aside with the aubergine slices to cool.

3 Transfer all the ingredients to a food processor and process just until a coarse purée forms. Transfer to a serving bowl and stir in the parsley. Taste and adjust the seasoning, if necessary. Serve at once, or cover and chill until 15 minutes before required. Sprinkle with paprika and serve with slices of French bread.

courgette fritters with yogurt dip

ingredients

SERVES 4

2–3 courgettes, about 400 g/
    14 oz
1 garlic clove, crushed
3 spring onions, finely sliced
125 g/4$^{1}/_{2}$ oz feta cheese,
    crumbled
2 tbsp finely chopped
    fresh parsley
2 tbsp finely chopped
    fresh mint
1 tbsp finely chopped fresh dill
$^{1}/_{2}$ tsp freshly grated nutmeg
2 tbsp all-purpose flour
pepper
2 eggs
2 tbsp olive oil
1 lemon, cut into quarters,
    to garnish

yogurt dip

250 g/9 oz strained plain
    yogurt
$^{1}/_{4}$ cucumber, diced
1 tbsp finely chopped fresh dill
pepper

method

1 Grate the courgettes straight onto a clean tea towel and cover with another. Pat well and set aside for 10 minutes until the courgettes are dry.

2 Meanwhile, to make the dip, mix the yogurt, cucumber, dill and pepper in a serving bowl. Cover and chill.

3 Tip the courgettes into a large mixing bowl. Stir in the garlic, spring onions, cheese, herbs, nutmeg, flour and pepper. Beat the eggs in a separate bowl and stir into the courgette mixture – the batter will be quite lumpy and uneven but this is fine.

4 Heat the oil in a large, wide frying pan over medium heat. Drop 4 tablespoonfuls of the batter into the pan, with space in between, and cook for 2–3 minutes on each side. Remove, drain on kitchen paper and keep warm. Cook the second batch of fritters in the same way. (There should be 8 fritters in total.)

5 Serve the fritters hot with the dip, garnished with lemon quarters.

vegetable soup with pesto

ingredients

SERVES 4

1 litre/32 fl oz fresh cold
    water
bouquet garni of 1 fresh parsley
    sprig, 1 fresh thyme sprig,
    and 1 bay leaf, tied together
    with clean string
2 celery stalks, chopped
3 baby leeks, chopped
4 baby carrots, chopped
150 g/5$\frac{1}{2}$ oz new potatoes,
    scrubbed and cut into
    bite-size chunks
4 tbsp shelled broad beans
    or peas
175 g/6 oz canned cannellini
    or flageolet beans, drained
    and rinsed
3 heads pak choi
150 g/5$\frac{1}{2}$ oz rocket
pepper

pesto

2 large handfuls fresh basil
    leaves
1 fresh green chilli, deseeded
2 garlic cloves
4 tbsp olive oil
1 tsp Parmesan cheese,
    finely grated

method

1 Put the water and bouquet garni into a large saucepan and add the celery, leeks, carrots and potatoes. Bring to the boil, then reduce the heat and simmer for 10 minutes.

2 Stir in the broad beans or peas and canned beans and simmer for a further 10 minutes. Stir in the pak choi and rocket, season with pepper and simmer for a further 2–3 minutes. Remove and discard the bouquet garni.

3 Meanwhile, to make the pesto, put the basil, chilli, garlic and oil into a food processor and pulse to form a thick paste. Stir in the cheese.

4 Stir most of the pesto into the soup, then ladle into warmed bowls. Top with the remaining pesto and serve at once.

sautéed garlic mushrooms

ingredients

SERVES 6

450 g/1 lb white mushrooms

5 tbsp Spanish olive oil

2 garlic cloves, finely chopped

squeeze of lemon juice

salt and pepper

4 tbsp chopped fresh flat-leaf
parsley, plus sprigs
to garnish

crusty bread, to serve

method

1 Wipe or brush clean the mushrooms, then trim off the stalks close to the caps. Cut any large mushrooms in half or into quarters. Heat the olive oil in a large, heavy-based frying pan, add the garlic and cook for 30 seconds–1 minute, or until lightly browned. Add the mushrooms and sauté over high heat, stirring most of the time, until the mushrooms have absorbed all the oil in the pan.

2 Reduce the heat to low. When the juices have come out of the mushrooms, increase the heat again, and sauté for 4–5 minutes, stirring most of the time, until the juices have almost evaporated. Add a squeeze of lemon juice and season to taste with salt and pepper. Stir in the chopped parsley and cook for a further minute.

3 Transfer the sautéed mushrooms to a warmed serving dish, garnish with the sprigs of parsley and serve piping hot or warm. Accompany with chunks or slices of crusty bread for mopping up the garlic cooking juices.

asparagus with melted butter

ingredients

SERVES 2

16–20 stalks of asparagus, trimmed to about 20 cm/8 inches

85 g/3 oz unsalted butter, melted

sea salt and pepper, to serve

method

1 Remove some of the base of the asparagus stalks with a potato peeler if they are rather thick. Tie the stalks together with string or use a wire basket so that they can easily be removed from the saucepan without damage.

2 Bring a large saucepan of salted water to the boil and plunge in the stalks. Cover with a lid and cook for 4–5 minutes. Pierce one stalk near the base with a sharp knife. If it is fairly soft remove from the heat at once. Do not overcook asparagus or the tender tips will fall off.

3 Drain the asparagus thoroughly and serve on large warmed plates with the butter poured over. Both the butter and the asparagus should be warm rather than hot. Serve with sea salt and pepper for sprinkling.

roasted pepper salad

ingredients

SERVES 8

3 red peppers

3 yellow peppers

5 tbsp Spanish extra virgin
    olive oil

2 tbsp dry sherry vinegar
    or lemon juice

2 garlic cloves, crushed

pinch of sugar

salt and pepper

1 tbsp capers

8 small black Spanish olives

2 tbsp chopped fresh
    marjoram, plus extra
    sprigs to garnish

method

1 Preheat the grill to high. Place the peppers on a wire rack or grill pan and cook under the grill for 10 minutes, until their skins have blackened and blistered, turning them frequently.

2 Remove the roasted peppers from the heat, and either put them in a bowl and immediately cover tightly with a clean, damp tea towel or put them in a plastic bag. The steam helps to soften the skins and makes it easier to remove them. Let stand for about 15 minutes, until cool enough to handle.

3 Holding one pepper at a time over a clean bowl, use a sharp knife to make a small hole in the base and gently squeeze out the juices and reserve them. Still holding the pepper over the bowl, carefully peel off the blackened skin with your fingers, or a knife, and discard it. Cut the peppers in half and remove the stem, core and seeds, then cut each pepper into neat thin strips. Arrange the pepper strips on a serving dish.

4 To the reserved pepper juices add the olive oil, sherry vinegar, garlic, sugar, salt and pepper. Whisk together until combined. Drizzle the dressing evenly over the salad.

5 Sprinkle the capers, olives and chopped marjoram over the salad, garnish with marjoram sprigs and serve at room temperature.

green bean salad with feta cheese

ingredients

SERVES 4

350 g/12 oz green beans

1 red onion, chopped

3–4 tbsp chopped fresh
    coriander

2 radishes, thinly sliced

75 g/2¾ oz feta cheese
    drained weight, crumbled

1 tsp chopped fresh oregano,
    plus extra leaves to garnish
    (optional)

pepper

2 tbsp red wine or fruit vinegar

80 ml/3 fl oz extra virgin
    olive oil

6 cherry tomatoes, halved

slices of crusty bread,
    to serve

method

1 Bring about 5 cm/2 inches of water to the boil in the bottom of a steamer. Add the beans to the top part of the steamer, cover and steam for 5 minutes, or until just tender.

2 Place the beans in a large bowl and add the onion, coriander, radishes and feta cheese.

3 Sprinkle the oregano over the salad, then season with pepper. Mix the vinegar and oil together in a small bowl and pour over the salad. Toss gently to mix well.

4 Transfer to a serving platter, surround with the tomato halves and serve at once with slices of crusty bread, or cover and chill until ready to serve.

warm red lentil salad with goat's cheese

ingredients

SERVES 4

2 tbsp olive oil

2 tsp cumin seeds

2 garlic cloves, crushed

2 tsp grated fresh root ginger

300 g/10^1/$_2$ oz split red lentils

750 ml/24 fl oz vegetable stock

2 tbsp chopped fresh mint

2 tbsp chopped fresh coriander

2 red onions, thinly sliced

200 g/7 oz baby spinach leaves

1 tsp hazelnut oil

150 g/5^1/$_2$ oz soft goat's cheese

4 tbsp Greek-style yogurt pepper

1 lemon, cut into quarters, to garnish

toasted rye bread, to serve

method

1 Heat half the olive oil in a large saucepan over medium heat, add the cumin seeds, garlic and ginger and cook for 2 minutes, stirring constantly.

2 Stir in the lentils, then add the stock, a ladleful at a time, until it is all absorbed, stirring constantly – this will take about 20 minutes. Remove from the heat and stir in the herbs.

3 Meanwhile, heat the remaining olive oil in a frying pan over medium heat, add the onions and cook, stirring frequently, for 10 minutes, or until soft and lightly browned.

4 Toss the spinach in the hazelnut oil in a bowl, then divide between 4 serving plates.

5 Mash the goat's cheese with the yogurt in a small bowl and season with pepper.

6 Divide the lentils between the serving plates and top with the onions and goat's cheese mixture. Garnish with lemon quarters and serve with toasted rye bread.

mexican three-bean chilli stew

ingredients

SERVES 6

140 g/5 oz each dried black
   beans, cannellini beans
   and borlotti beans, soaked
   overnight in separate
   bowls in water to cover
2 tbsp olive oil
1 large onion, finely chopped
2 red peppers, deseeded and
   diced
2 garlic cloves, very finely
   chopped
$1/2$ tsp cumin seeds, crushed
1 tsp coriander seeds,
   crushed
1 tsp dried oregano
$1/2$–2 tsp chilli powder
3 tbsp tomato purée
800 g/1 lb 12 oz canned
   chopped tomatoes
1 tsp sugar
1 tsp salt
625 ml/20 fl oz vegetable
   stock
3 tbsp chopped fresh
   coriander
slices of red onion and small
   pieces of avocado,
   to garnish

method

1 Drain the beans, put in separate saucepans and cover with cold water. Bring to the boil and boil vigorously for 10–15 minutes, then reduce the heat and simmer for 35–45 minutes until just tender. Drain and set aside.

2 Heat the oil in a large, heavy-based saucepan over medium heat. Add the onion and peppers and cook, stirring frequently, for 5 minutes, or until softened.

3 Add the garlic, cumin and coriander seeds and oregano and cook, stirring, for 30 seconds until the garlic is beginning to colour. Add the chilli powder and tomato purée and cook, stirring, for 1 minute. Add the tomatoes, sugar, salt, beans and stock. Bring to the boil, then reduce the heat, cover and simmer, stirring occasionally, for 45 minutes.

4 Stir in the fresh coriander. Ladle into individual warmed bowls and serve at once. Garnish with slices of red onion and small pieces of avocado.

kidney bean risotto

ingredients

SERVES 4

4 tbsp olive oil

1 onion, chopped

2 garlic cloves, finely chopped

175 g/6 oz brown rice

625 ml/20 fl oz vegetable
    stock

salt and pepper

1 red pepper, deseeded
    and chopped

2 celery stalks, sliced

225 g/8 oz chestnut
    mushrooms, thinly sliced

425 g/15 oz canned red
    kidney beans, drained
    and rinsed

3 tbsp chopped fresh parsley,
    plus extra to garnish

55 g/2 oz cashews

method

1 Heat half the oil in a large, heavy-based saucepan. Add the onion and cook, stirring occasionally, for 5 minutes, or until softened. Add half the garlic and cook, stirring frequently, for 2 minutes, then add the rice and stir for 1 minute, or until the grains are thoroughly coated with the oil.

2 Add the stock and a pinch of salt and bring to the boil, stirring constantly. Reduce the heat, cover and simmer for 35–40 minutes, or until all the liquid has been absorbed.

3 Meanwhile, heat the remaining oil in a heavy-based frying pan. Add the pepper and celery and cook, stirring frequently, for 5 minutes. Add the sliced mushrooms and the remaining garlic and cook, stirring frequently, for 4–5 minutes.

4 Stir the rice into the frying pan. Add the beans, parsley and cashews. Season with salt and pepper and cook, stirring constantly, until hot. Transfer to a warmed serving dish, sprinkle with extra parsley, and serve at once.

spinach with chickpeas

ingredients

SERVES 4–6

2 tbsp olive oil

1 large garlic clove, cut in half

1 medium onion,
   chopped finely

$1/2$ tsp cumin

pinch cayenne pepper

pinch turmeric

800 g/1 lb 12 oz canned
   chickpeas, drained
   and rinsed

500 g/18 oz baby spinach
   leaves, rinsed and
   shaken dry

2 pimientos del piquillo,
   drained and sliced

salt and pepper

method

1 Heat the oil in a large, lidded frying pan over medium–high heat. Add the garlic and cook for 2 minutes, or until golden but not brown. Remove with a slotted spoon and discard.

2 Add the onion and cumin, cayenne and turmeric and cook, stirring, for about 5 minutes until soft. Add the chickpeas and stir around until they are lightly coloured with the turmeric and cayenne.

3 Stir in the spinach with just the water clinging to its leaves. Cover and cook for 4–5 minutes until wilted. Uncover, stir in the pimientos del piquillo and continue cooking, stirring gently, until all the liquid evaporates. Season with salt and pepper and serve.

vegetable & hazelnut loaf

ingredients

SERVES 4

2 tbsp sunflower oil, plus
    extra for oiling

1 onion, chopped

1 garlic clove, finely chopped

2 celery stalks, chopped

1 tbsp plain flour

200 ml/7 fl oz strained
    canned tomatoes

115 g/4 oz fresh wholemeal
    breadcrumbs

2 carrots, grated

115 g/4 oz toasted hazelnuts,
    ground

1 tbsp dark soy sauce

2 tbsp chopped fresh
    coriander

1 egg, lightly beaten

salt and pepper

mixed red and green lettuce
    leaves, to serve

method

1 Oil and line a 450-g/1-lb loaf pan. Heat the oil in a heavy-based frying pan over medium heat. Add the onion and cook, stirring frequently, for 5 minutes, or until softened. Add the garlic and celery and cook, stirring frequently, for 5 minutes. Add the flour and cook, stirring constantly, for 1 minute. Gradually stir in the strained canned tomatoes and cook, stirring constantly, until thickened. Remove the pan from the heat.

2 Put the breadcrumbs, carrots, ground hazelnuts, soy sauce and coriander in a bowl. Add the tomato mixture and stir well. Cool slightly, then beat in the egg and season with salt and pepper.

3 Spoon the mixture into the prepared pan and smooth the surface. Cover with foil and bake in a preheated oven, 180°C/350°F/Gas Mark 4, for 1 hour. If serving hot, turn the loaf out on to a warmed serving dish and serve immediately with mixed red and green salad leaves. Alternatively, cool the loaf in the pan before turning out.

vegetarian lasagne

ingredients

SERVES 4

olive oil, for brushing

2 aubergines, sliced

2 tbsp butter

1 garlic clove, finely chopped

4 courgettes, sliced

1 tbsp finely chopped fresh
    flat-leaf parsley

1 tbsp finely chopped fresh
    marjoram

225 g/8 oz mozzarella
    cheese, grated

625 ml/20 fl oz strained
    canned tomatoes

175 g/6 oz dried no-precook
    lasagne sheets

salt and pepper

béchamel sauce (see below)

55 g/2 oz freshly grated
    Parmesan cheese

béchamel sauce

300 ml/10 fl oz milk

1 bay leaf

6 black peppercorns

slice of onion

mace blade

2 tbsp butter

3 tbsp plain flour

salt and pepper

method

1 To make the béchamel sauce, pour the milk into a saucepan. Add the bay leaf, peppercorns, onion and mace. Heat to just below boiling point, then remove from the heat, cover, infuse for 10 minutes, then strain. Melt the butter in a separate saucepan. Sprinkle in the flour and cook over low heat, stirring constantly, for 1 minute. Gradually stir in the milk, then bring to the boil and cook, stirring, until thickened and smooth. Season with salt and pepper.

2 Brush a grill pan with olive oil and heat until smoking. Add half the aubergine slices and cook over medium heat for 8 minutes, or until golden brown all over. Remove from the grill pan and drain on kitchen paper. Repeat with the remaining aubergine slices.

3 Melt the butter in a frying pan and add the garlic, courgettes, parsley and marjoram. Cook over medium heat, stirring frequently, for 5 minutes, or until the courgettes are golden all over. Remove and drain on kitchen paper.

4 Layer the aubergine, courgettes, mozzarella, tomatoes and lasagne in an ovenproof dish brushed with olive oil, seasoning as you go and finishing with a layer of lasagne. Pour over the béchamel sauce, making sure that all the pasta is covered. Sprinkle with Parmesan cheese and bake in a preheated oven, 200°C/400°F/Gas Mark 6, for 30–40 minutes, or until golden brown. Serve at once.

chilli broccoli pasta

ingredients

SERVES 4

225 g/8 oz dried penne or
    macaroni

225 g/8 oz broccoli, cut into
    florets

50 ml/2 fl oz extra virgin
    olive oil

2 large garlic cloves, chopped

2 fresh red chillies, deseeded
    and diced

8 cherry tomatoes (optional)

fresh basil leaves, to garnish

method

1 Bring a large saucepan of salted boiling water to the boil. Add the pasta, return to the boil and cook for 8–10 minutes until tender but still firm to the bite. Drain the pasta, refresh under cold running water and drain again. Set aside.

2 Bring a separate saucepan of salted water to the boil, add the broccoli and cook for 5 minutes. Drain, refresh under cold running water and drain again.

3 Heat the oil, in the pan that the pasta was cooked in, over high heat. Add the garlic, chillies and tomatoes, if using, and cook, stirring, for 1 minute.

4 Add the broccoli and mix well. Cook for 2 minutes, stirring, to heat through. Add the pasta and mix well again. Cook for a further minute. Transfer the pasta to a large, warmed serving bowl and serve garnished with basil leaves.

sweet-&-sour vegetables with cashews

ingredients

SERVES 4

1 tbsp vegetable or peanut oil

1 tsp chilli oil

2 onions, sliced

2 carrots, thinly sliced

2 courgettes, thinly sliced

115 g/4 oz broccoli,
  cut into florets

115 g/4 oz white mushrooms,
  sliced

115 g/4 oz small pak choi,
  halved

2 tbsp jaggery or brown sugar

2 tbsp Thai soy sauce

1 tbsp rice vinegar

55 g/2 oz cashews

method

1 Heat both the oils in a preheated wok or frying pan, add the onions, and stir-fry for 1–2 minutes until beginning to soften.

2 Add the carrots, courgettes and broccoli and stir-fry for 2–3 minutes. Add the mushrooms, pak choi, sugar, soy sauce and vinegar and stir-fry for 1–2 minutes.

3 Meanwhile, heat a dry, heavy-based frying pan over high heat, add the cashews and cook, shaking the pan frequently, until lightly toasted. Sprinkle the cashews over the stir-fry and serve immediately.

creamy spinach & mushroom pasta

ingredients

SERVES 4

300 g/10^1/$_2$ oz dried penne or
    pasta of your choice
2 tbsp olive oil
250 g/9 oz mushrooms, sliced
1 tsp dried oregano
275 ml/9 fl oz vegetable stock
1 tbsp lemon juice
6 tbsp cream cheese
200 g/7 oz frozen spinach
    leaves
salt and pepper

method

1 Cook the pasta in a large pan of lightly salted boiling water, according to the packet instructions. Drain, reserving 175 ml/6 fl oz of the cooking liquid.

2 Meanwhile, heat the oil in a large, heavy-based frying pan over medium heat, add the mushrooms and cook, stirring frequently, for 8 minutes, or until almost crisp. Stir in the oregano, stock and lemon juice and cook for 10–12 minutes, or until the sauce is reduced by half.

3 Stir in the cream cheese and spinach and cook over medium–low heat for 3–5 minutes. Add the reserved cooking liquid, then the cooked pasta. Stir well, season to taste with salt and pepper and heat through gently before serving.

roasted garlic creamed potatoes

ingredients

SERVES 4

2 whole garlic bulbs

1 tbsp olive oil

900 g/2 lb floury potatoes,
    peeled

125 ml/4 fl oz milk

55 g/2 oz butter

salt and pepper

method

1 Separate the garlic cloves, place on a large piece of foil and drizzle with the oil. Wrap the garlic in the foil and roast in a preheated oven, 180°C/350°F/Gas Mark 4, for about 1 hour, or until very tender. Let cool slightly.

2 Meanwhile, cut the potatoes into chunks, then cook in a saucepan of lightly salted boiling water for 15 minutes, or until tender.

3 Squeeze the cooled garlic cloves out of their skins and push through a sieve into a saucepan. Add the milk and butter and season with salt and pepper. Heat gently until the butter has melted.

4 Drain the cooked potatoes, then mash in the pan until smooth. Pour in the garlic mixture and heat gently, stirring, until the ingredients are combined. Serve hot.

caramelized onion tart

ingredients

SERVES 4–6

7 tbsp unsalted butter

600 g/1 lb 5 oz onions,
    thinly sliced

2 eggs

100 ml/3^1/$_2$ fl oz double
    cream

salt and pepper

100 g/3^1/$_2$ oz grated Gruyère
    cheese

20-cm/8-inch ready-baked
    pastry case

100 g/3^1/$_2$ oz coarsely grated
    Parmesan cheese

method

1 Melt the butter in a heavy-based frying pan over medium heat. Add the onions and cook, stirring frequently to avoid burning, for 30 minutes, or until well-browned and caramelized. Remove the onions from the pan and set aside.

2 Beat the eggs in a large bowl, stir in the cream and season to taste with salt and pepper. Add the Gruyère and mix well. Stir in the cooked onions.

3 Pour the egg and onion mixture into the baked pastry case and sprinkle with the Parmesan cheese. Place on a baking sheet. Bake in a preheated oven, 190°C/375°F/Gas Mark 5, for 15–20 minutes until the filling has set and begun to brown.

4 Remove from the oven and let rest for at least 10 minutes. The tart can be served hot or left to cool to room temperature.

stir-fried rice with green vegetables

ingredients

SERVES 4

225 g/8 oz jasmine rice

2 tbsp vegetable or peanut oil

1 tbsp green curry paste

6 spring onions, sliced

2 garlic cloves, crushed

1 courgette, cut into thin
    sticks

115 g/4 oz green beans

175 g/6 oz asparagus,
    trimmed

3–4 fresh Thai basil leaves

method

1 Cook the rice in lightly salted boiling water for 12–15 minutes, drain well, then cool thoroughly and chill overnight.

2 Heat the oil in a wok and stir-fry the curry paste for 1 minute. Add the spring onions and garlic and stir-fry for 1 minute.

3 Add the courgette, beans and asparagus and stir-fry for 3–4 minutes, until just tender. Break up the rice and add it to the wok. Cook, stirring constantly for 2–3 minutes, until the rice is hot. Stir in the basil leaves. Serve hot.

greek salad

ingredients

SERVES 4

4 tomatoes, cut into wedges

1 onion, sliced

$^1/_2$ cucumber, sliced

225 g/8 oz kalamata olives,
    stoned

225 g/8 oz feta cheese,
    cubed

2 tbsp fresh coriander leaves

fresh flat-leaf parsley sprigs,
    to garnish

pitta bread, to serve

dressing

5 tbsp extra virgin olive oil

2 tbsp white wine vinegar

1 tbsp lemon juice

$^1/_2$ tsp sugar

1 tbsp chopped fresh
    coriander

salt and pepper

method

1 To make the dressing, put all the ingredients for the dressing into a large bowl and mix well together.

2 Add the tomatoes, onion, cucumber, olives, cheese and coriander. Toss all the ingredients together, then divide between individual serving bowls. Garnish with parsley sprigs and serve with pitta bread.

stuffed red peppers with basil

ingredients

SERVES 4

140 g/5 oz long-grain
   white or brown rice
4 large red peppers
2 tbsp olive oil
1 garlic clove, chopped
4 shallots, chopped
1 celery stalk, chopped
3 tbsp chopped
   toasted walnuts
2 tomatoes, peeled
   and chopped
1 tbsp lemon juice
50 g/1^3/$_4$ oz raisins
4 tbsp freshly grated
   Cheddar cheese
2 tbsp chopped fresh basil
salt and pepper
fresh basil sprigs, to garnish
lemon wedges, to serve

method

1 Cook the rice in a pan of lightly salted boiling water for 20 minutes, if using white rice, or 35 minutes, if using brown. Drain, rinse under cold running water, then drain again.

2 Using a sharp knife, cut the tops off the peppers and set aside. Remove the seeds and white cores, then blanch the peppers and reserved tops in boiling water for 2 minutes. Remove from the heat and drain well. Heat half the oil in a large frying pan. Add the garlic and shallots and cook, stirring, for 3 minutes. Add the celery, walnuts, tomatoes, lemon juice and raisins and cook for a further 5 minutes. Remove from the heat and stir in the cheese, chopped basil, salt and pepper.

3 Stuff the peppers with the rice mixture and arrange them in a baking dish. Place the tops on the peppers, drizzle over the remaining oil, loosely cover with foil, and bake in a preheated oven, 180°C/350°F/Gas Mark 4, for 45 minutes. Remove from the oven, garnish with basil sprigs and serve with lemon wedges.

potato-topped vegetables

ingredients

SERVES 4

1 carrot, diced

175 g/6 oz cauliflower florets

175 g/6 oz broccoli florets

1 fennel bulb, sliced

75 g/2^3/$_4$ oz green beans,
    halved

2 tbsp butter

2^1/$_2$ tbsp plain flour

150 ml/5 fl oz vegetable stock

150 ml/5 fl oz dry white wine

150 ml/5 fl oz milk

175 g/6 oz chestnut
    mushrooms, cut into
    quarters

2 tbsp chopped fresh sage

salt and pepper

topping

900 g/2 lb diced floury
    potatoes

2 tbsp butter

4 tbsp plain yogurt

75 g/2^1/$_2$ oz freshly grated
    Parmesan cheese

1 tsp fennel seeds

method

1 Cook the carrot, cauliflower, broccoli, fennel and beans in a large saucepan of boiling water for 10 minutes, until just tender. Drain the vegetables thoroughly and set aside.

2 Melt the butter in a saucepan. Stir in the flour and cook for 1 minute. Remove from the heat and stir in the stock, wine and milk. Return to the heat and bring to the boil, stirring until thickened. Stir in the reserved vegetables, mushrooms and sage and season with salt and pepper.

3 Meanwhile, make the topping. Cook the diced potatoes in a saucepan of boiling water for 10–15 minutes. Drain and mash with the butter, yogurt and half the Parmesan cheese. Stir in the fennel seeds.

4 Spoon the vegetable mixture into a 1-litre/ 32-fl oz pie dish. Spoon the potato over the top and sprinkle with the remaining cheese. Cook in a preheated oven, 190°C/375°F/Gas Mark 5, for 30–35 minutes, until golden.

stuffed baked potatoes

ingredients

SERVES 4

900 g/2 lb baking potatoes,
    scrubbed

2 tbsp vegetable oil

1 tsp coarse sea salt

115 g/4 oz butter

1 small onion, chopped

salt and pepper

115 g/4 oz grated Cheddar
    cheese or crumbled
    Stilton cheese

snipped fresh chives,
    to garnish

optional

4 tbsp canned, drained
    corn kernels

4 tbsp cooked mushrooms,
    courgettes or peppers

method

1 Prick the potatoes in several places with a fork and put on a baking sheet. Brush with the oil and sprinkle with the salt. Bake in a preheated oven, 190°C/375°F/Gas Mark 5, for 1 hour, or until the skins are crispy and the insides are soft when pierced with a fork.

2 Meanwhile, melt 1 tablespoon of the butter in a small frying pan over medium–low heat. Add the onion and cook, stirring occasionally, for 8–10 minutes until soft and golden. Set aside.

3 Cut the potatoes in half lengthways. Scoop the flesh into a large bowl, leaving the skins intact. Set aside the skins. Increase the oven temperature to 200°C/400°F/Gas Mark 6.

4 Coarsely mash the potato flesh and mix in the onion and remaining butter. Add salt and pepper to taste and stir in any of the optional ingredients. Spoon the mixture back into the reserved potato skins. Top with the cheese.

5 Cook the filled potato skins in the oven for 10 minutes, or until the cheese has melted and is beginning to brown. Garnish with chives and serve immediately.

This edition published by Parragon in 2008

Parragon
Queen Street House
4 Queen Street
Bath BA1 1HE, UK

Copyright © Parragon Books Ltd 2007

ISBN 978-1-4075-3091-8

Printed in China

Notes for the reader
• This book uses both metric and imperial measurements. Follow the same units of measurement throughout; do not mix metric and imperial. All spoon measurements are level: teaspoons are assumed to be 5 ml, and tablespoons are assumed to be 15 ml. Unless otherwise stated, milk is assumed to be full fat, eggs and individual vegetables are medium, and pepper is freshly ground black pepper.
• The times given are an approximate guide only. Preparation times differ according to the techniques used by different people and the cooking times may also vary from those given. Optional ingredients, variations or serving suggestions have not been included in the calculations.
• Recipes using raw or very lightly cooked eggs should be avoided by infants, the elderly, pregnant women, convalescents and anyone suffering from an illness. Pregnant and breastfeeding women are advised to avoid eating peanuts and peanut products. Sufferers from nut allergies should be aware that some of the ready-made ingredients used in the recipes in this book may contain nuts. Always check the packaging before use.